The Joy of Second-Year Piano

THE JOY OF SECOND-YEAR PIANO follows on from the immensely popular FIRST-YEAR book. Its purpose is to provide competent beginners of all ages with the repertory and guidance to develop new skills as they reinforce fundamental techniques. The pieces have been selected carefully and sequenced progressively, with an emphasis on repetition of learned skills. The book can be worked through piece by piece, however some students may advance quickly enough to skip the shorter, simpler pieces.

The opening pages offer some basic new information for the student to refer to, though the best learning experience will be achieved through involvement and direct interaction with their teacher.

Tell me, I forget.
Show me, I remember.
Involve me, I understand.

In addition to the introductory tutorial pages, helpful notes can be found throughout, bringing to attention new concepts and techniques for the student and teacher to discuss. Warm-up exercises have been specially written with particular techniques or pieces in mind, and these can be found on pages 9–11. It is recommended that teachers highlight the significance of these exercises to ensure the student fully appreciates their purpose and the benefits of practice.

THE JOY OF SECOND-YEAR PIANO includes well-known classical favorites by the most prominent composers, and students will likely have heard many of these. A shrewd teacher will inspire their student to listen to these pieces well in advance of learning them, as this will encourage the student to recognise musical features and notice mistakes as they happen.

This book aims to engage and stimulate the student's interest, guide them toward developing a sound musical taste, motivate further study and, in general, foster the love of music.

We hope that THE JOY OF SECOND-YEAR PIANO fulfils these goals.

YORKTOWN MUSIC PRESS/MUSIC SALES LIMITED
London/New York/Paris/Sydney/Copenhagen/Berlin/Madrid/Hong Kong/Tokyo

Contents

Note Guide

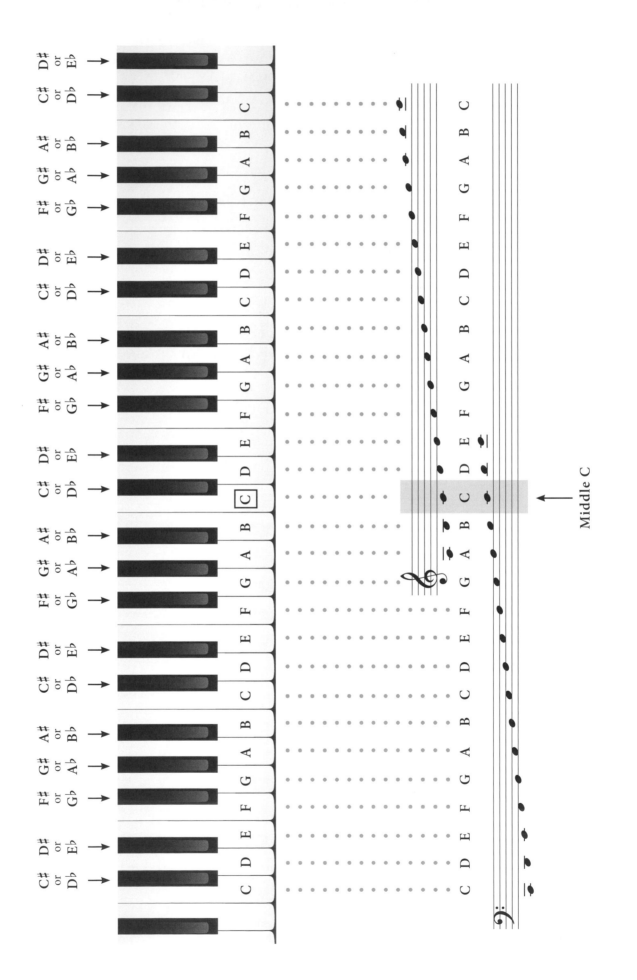

Middle C

A few reminders before you begin…

Sitting at your piano

Sit facing the middle of the keyboard with both feet firmly on the floor in front of the pedals.

Allow the upper arm to hang loosely. When you play, make sure your elbows are at the same level as your hands on the keyboard, so that your forearms are parallel to the floor.

You may be able to adjust the height of your stool or put a cushion on your chair so that you are sitting at the best level to play.

Always try to keep your arms and hands relaxed when playing.

Hand position

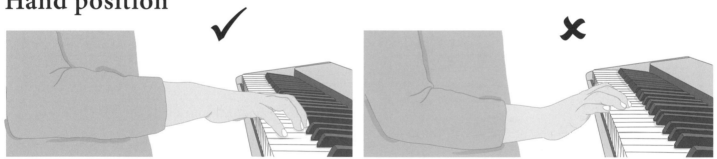

When you play, your hand should be cupped, as if you're holding a small ball. Gently curve your fingers nicely and play with your fingertips, not your nails.

Don't let your wrist drop below the level of your knuckles, and remember to keep your hand and arm relaxed.

Fingering numbers

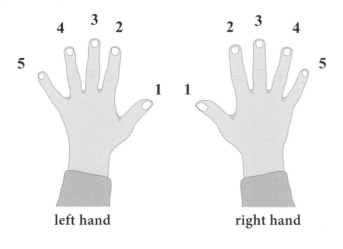

left hand   right hand

Your fingers are given numbers from 1 to 5, starting with your thumbs and numbering outwards.

Fingering is sometimes written above or below notes to help you move your hands around the keyboard efficiently.

The Grand Staff

Music for the piano or keyboard is usually written on a **grand staff**—two staves joined by a **brace**.

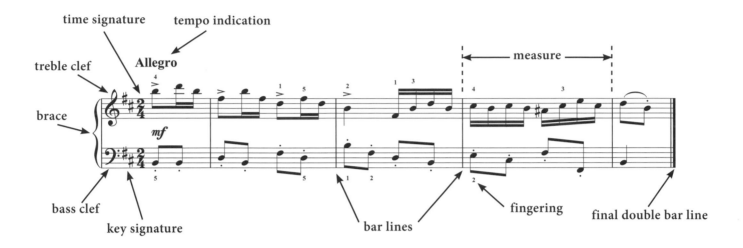

Notes on the upper stave, beginning with the **treble clef**, are usually played by the right hand.

Notes on the lower stave, beginning with the **bass clef**, are usually played by the left hand.

The music is divided by **bar lines** into **measures**. Usually, each measure contains the same number of beats (or counts), as indicated by the **time signature** at the beginning of the music. The speed or **tempo** is often indicated at the start of the piece, traditionally in Italian but sometimes in other languages.

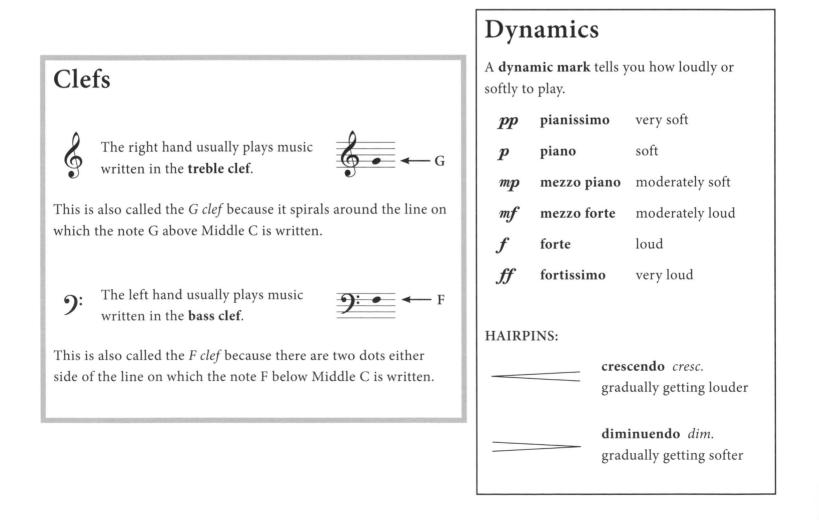

Clefs

The right hand usually plays music written in the **treble clef**.

This is also called the *G clef* because it spirals around the line on which the note G above Middle C is written.

The left hand usually plays music written in the **bass clef**.

This is also called the *F clef* because there are two dots either side of the line on which the note F below Middle C is written.

Dynamics

A **dynamic mark** tells you how loudly or softly to play.

pp	**pianissimo**	very soft
p	**piano**	soft
mp	**mezzo piano**	moderately soft
mf	**mezzo forte**	moderately loud
f	**forte**	loud
ff	**fortissimo**	very loud

HAIRPINS:

crescendo *cresc.*
gradually getting louder

diminuendo *dim.*
gradually getting softer

Note values and their rests

The note value tells you the duration of a note—how many beats or **counts** it lasts. When read in sequence, note values show the **rhythm** of the music.

Each has its own **rest**, which indicates a silence for the equivalent duration.

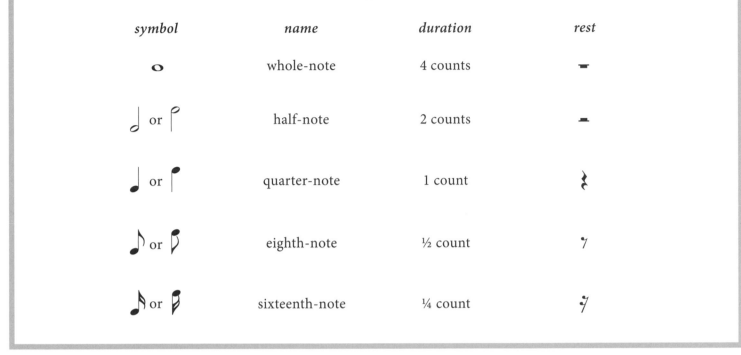

symbol	name	duration	rest
o	whole-note	4 counts	▬
♩ or ⌐	half-note	2 counts	▬
♩ or ⌐	quarter-note	1 count	⸾
♪ or ♪	eighth-note	½ count	⸵
♬ or ♬	sixteenth-note	¼ count	⸶

Beaming

A **beam** is often used to join note values of an *eighth-note* or shorter to show a rhythmic grouping.

The most common grouping indicates *quarter-note* beats (one count), which can help show where the beats of the measure fall.

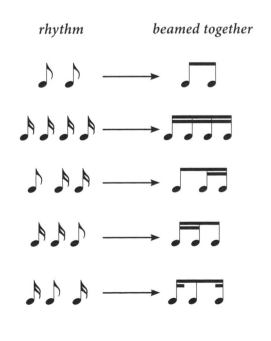

rhythm *beamed together*

Dotted rhythms

A **dotted note** lasts for 1½ times its usual duration.

symbol	name	duration	rest
♩. or ⌐.	dotted half-note	3 counts	▬.
♩. or ⌐.	dotted quarter-note	1½ counts	⸾.
♪. or ♪.	dotted eighth-note	¾ count	⸵.

Triplets

A **triplet** is a subdivision of a beat or beats into three notes of equal duration.

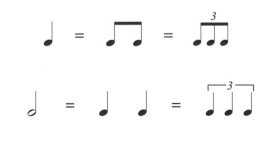

Time Signatures

The **time signature** appears after the key signature at the beginning of the music.

The *upper* figure shows the number of counts in each measure and the *lower* figure tells us what note duration gets one count.

4/4 or **C** = four quarter-note counts per measure (also called **common time**)

2/2 or **¢** = two half-note counts per measure (also called **cut time** or **cut common time**)

3/4 = three quarter-note counts per measure

6/8 = six eighth-note counts per measure, grouped in two groups of three

This **compound meter** has a pulse of two dotted quarter-notes per measure.

2/4 = two quarter-note counts per measure

Sharps, flats and naturals

♯   A **sharp** sign *raises the pitch of a note by a semitone* to the very next key on the right.

♭   A **flat** sign *lowers the pitch of a note by a semitone* to the very next key on the left.

♮   A **natural** sign *cancels the effect of a sharp or a flat*, representing the unaltered pitch.

Refer to the **Note Guide** on page 4 to see how this works. In general, the white keys are **natural** notes and the black keys are **sharp** or **flat** notes.

Key signatures and accidentals

A **key signature** is written at the start of each line of music. It tells us which notes should be played as *sharps* or *flats* which is easier than writing a ♯ or ♭ sign every time these notes appear.

An **accidental** is a *sharp, flat* or *natural* sign placed in front of a note to alter the pitch and produce a note that isn't in the key signature. The accidental affects all following notes of that pitch for the remainder of the measure.

Warm-up exercises...

These warm-ups introduce some of the techniques that you'll encounter as you progress through this book.

Practise them hands separately at first. When you put hands together, begin slowly, and as you master how to play the exercise, gradually build up your speed.

WARM-UP 1: This is a warm-up for your left hand only. Watch out for the clef changes.

WARM-UP 2: First play this *p* and then *f*.

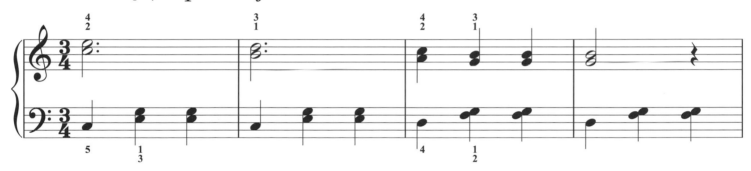

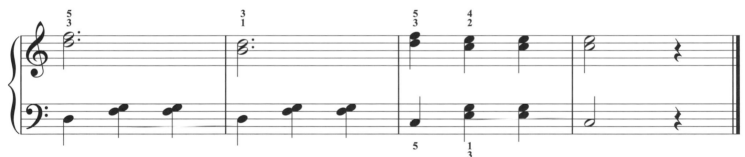

WARM-UP 3: Watch out for finger-crossing in this exercise — your second finger should move over your thumb.

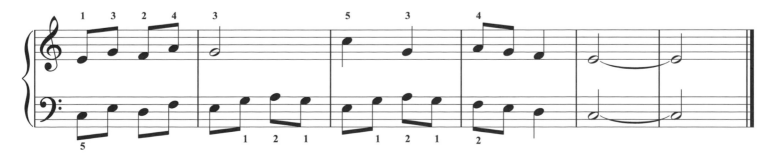

WARM-UP 4: Make sure all the 3-note chords are sounded evenly and together.

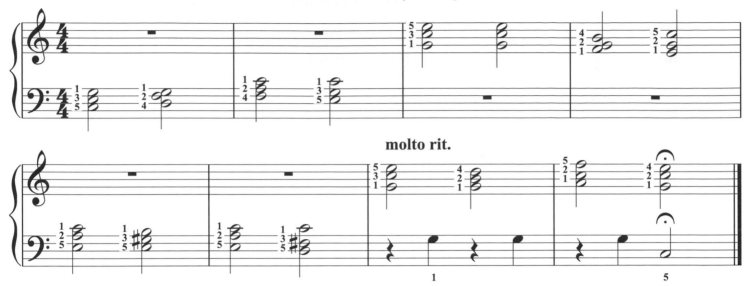

WARM-UP 5: Look at the time signature before you play—count two half-notes in each measure.
Play smoothly *(legato)* and watch out for both parallel and contrary motion between the hands.

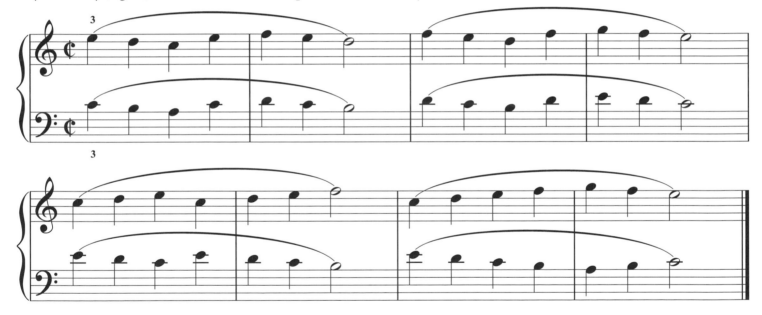

WARM-UP 6: Practise hands separately until you are confident. Your right hand has to stretch increasingly larger intervals.

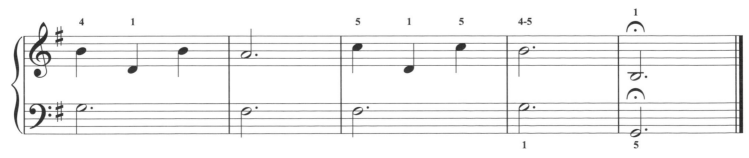

WARM-UP 7: There are many different rhythms in this warm-up. Practise the right hand on its own first.
Watch out for the different articulations—there are **staccato** dots, **tenuto** marks and **accented staccato** marks.

WARM-UP 8: Use this exercise to practise finger control. Make sure your thumbs are not too heavy and bring out the three separate lines.

WARM-UP 9: Play this warm-up smoothly *(legato)*, keeping the independent left hand steady and even.

Your left hand plays an **ostinato** for most of this piece. Practise it on its own until you can play it confidently, keeping a steady pulse, without thinking about it too much. Then you can concentrate on the right hand.

Make sure you **accent** the notes where marked.

Pow Wow

Marie Hill

With a steady beat

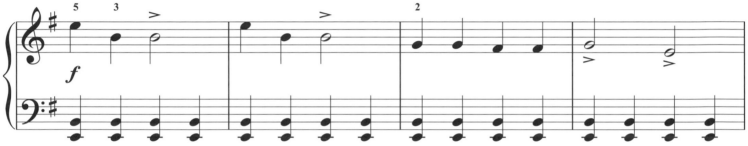

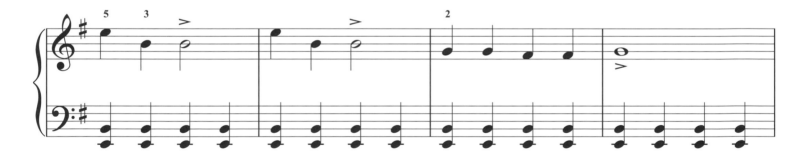

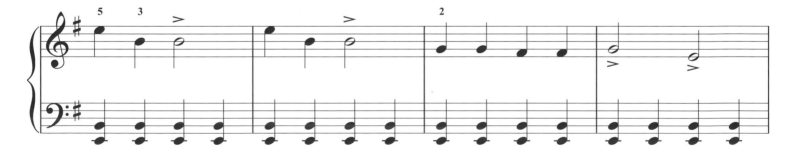

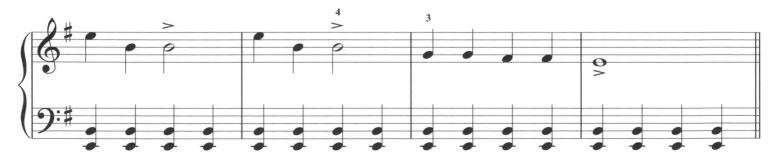

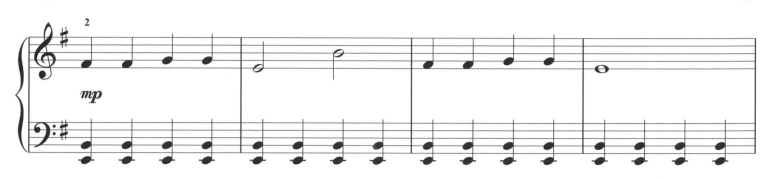

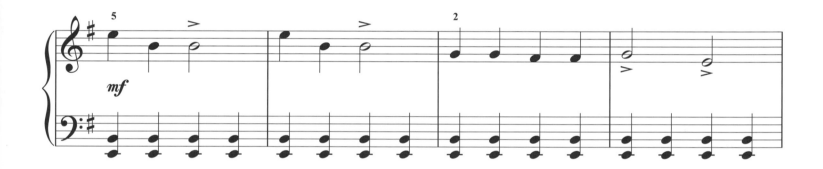

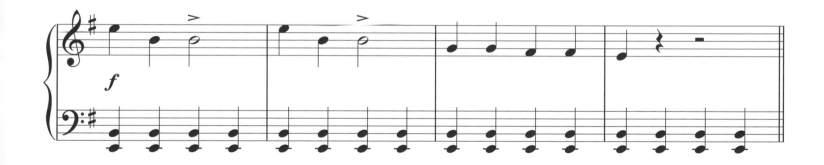

Practise this left-hand progression until you are comfortable with the movement:
Try Warm-ups 1 and 2 on page 9 to prepare.

The Hunters' Song

Cornelius Gurlitt

Con moto

poco rit.

cresc.

A tempo

Practise the right hand on its own at first, using the **phrase marks** or **slurs** to help you to play expressively, joining notes of one phrase into a smooth line.

The Italian word *smorzando* tells you to get quieter and slower very gradually, fading to nothing.

Try Warm-up 1 on page 9 to prepare.

Former Friends

No. 3 from FOR CHILDREN

Béla Bartók

Andante

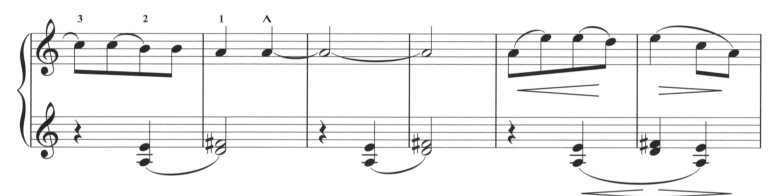

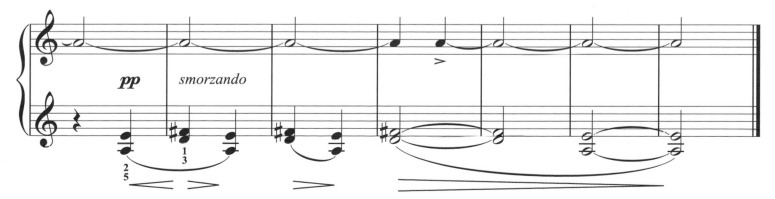

Watch for the changes of hand position in this song. Use the **hairpins** to add expression to your performance: *crescendo* getting gradually louder, and *diminuendo* getting gradually quieter.

Long, Long Ago

Thomas H. Bayley

Now you are come, all my grief is re - moved,

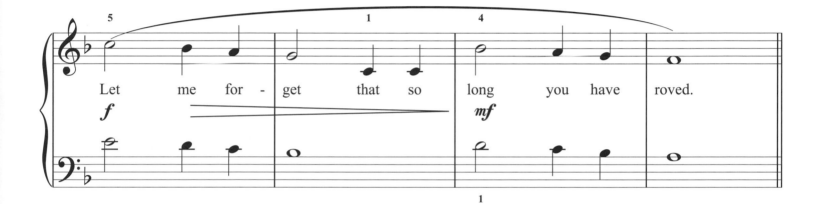

Let me for - get that so long you have roved.

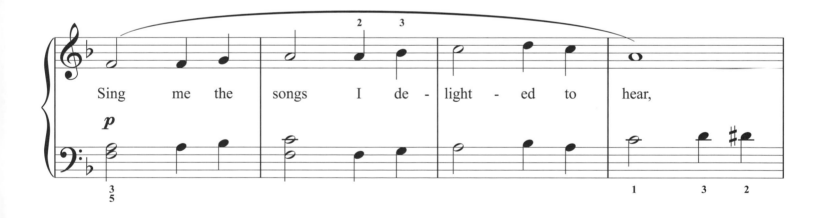

Sing me the songs I de - light - ed to hear,

Slower and softer

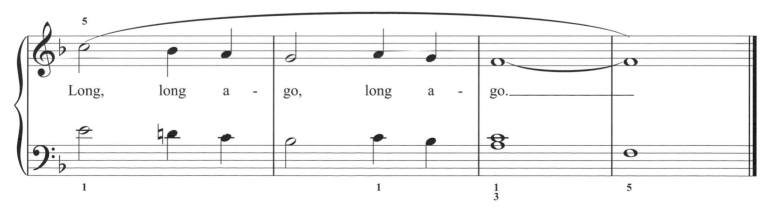

Long, long a - go, long a - go.

18

Prepare for this by playing Warm-up 3 on page 9 to help you with the left-hand fingering.

D.C. al Fine tells you to repeat from the beginning up until the point marked **Fine** (pronounced 'Feenay').

Little Birdie In A Tree

Moderately

Traditional English

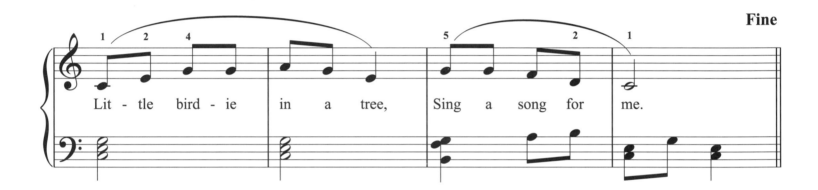

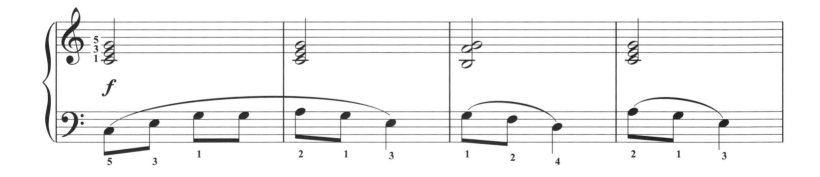

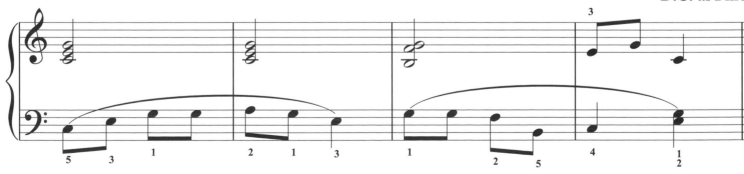

This piece begins on the third beat of the bar—an **upbeat**. Keep the left-hand chords *staccato* throughout and make sure all three notes are sounded together. Try Warm-up 4 on page 10 to prepare.

Quadrille

Franz Joseph Haydn

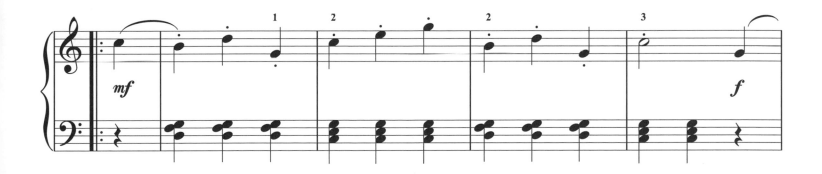

This song begins on the fourth beat of the bar—an **upbeat**. Watch out for the dotted quarter-note rhythms. Count carefully as you play. Don't forget to slow down a lot at the end, where **molto rit.** is marked.

Prepare by playing Warm-up 4 on page 10.

America, The Beautiful

Words by Kathleen L. Bates
Music by Samuel A. Ward

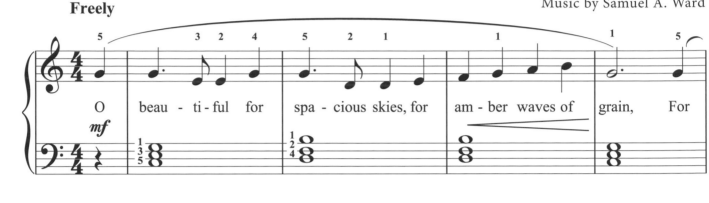

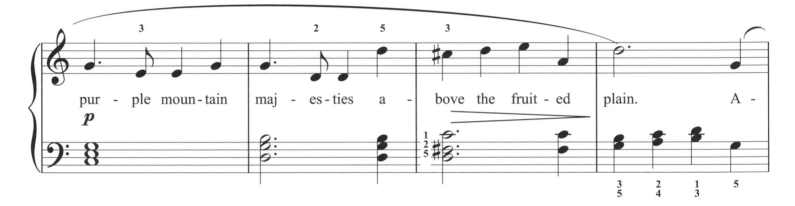

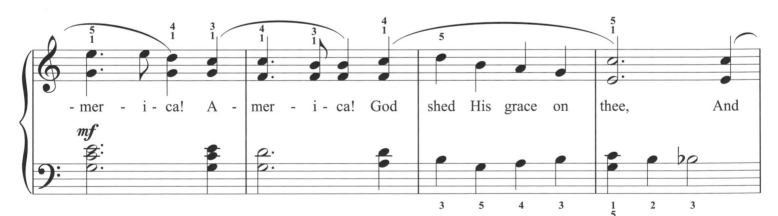

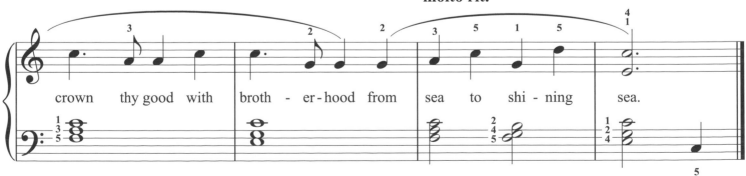

Prepare for the parallel and contrary motion in this piece using Warm-up 5 on page 10.

Look at the **time signature** at the start. It is known as **cut time** or **cut common time** and tells you there are two half-note counts in each measure. It is usually used for pieces at a quick, march-like tempo.

Practise hands separately at first. When you feel confident, practise measures 1–2 and 9–10 hands together several times before playing from the beginning.

Gavotta

James Hook

Look at the **key signature** for this piece—all Fs are to be played as F♯s.

Also watch out for the **accidentals** (a sharp sign before the C in measures 2, 3 *etc.*). An accidental affects all notes of that pitch that follow in that measure.

Là ci darem la mano
from DON GIOVANNI

Wolfgang Amadeus Mozart

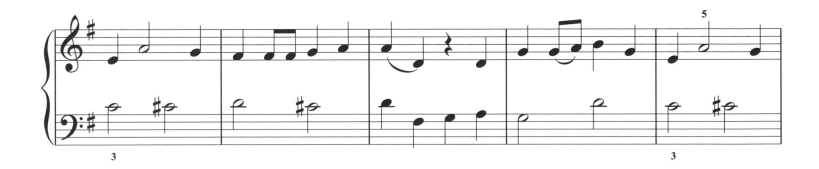

This song begins on an **upbeat**. Count carefully to help you play the rhythms correctly.

The symbol on the last chord is called a **fermata** and tells you to pause, holding the notes for longer than their written duration.

Oh! Susanna

Stephen Foster

24

Practise the left hand on its own to begin with — it moves in both **parallel** and **contrary motion** with the right hand. Also, when playing the 2-note and 3-note chords, make sure you sound all notes of the chord together.

Notice that the C♯ in measure 3 is the same note as the D♭ in measure 12. Prepare for this using Warm-up 5 on page 10.

Polly, Put The Kettle On

Quickly

Traditional English

There are three types of articulation to perform here—**staccato** ♩   **accent** ♩   **tenuto** ♩

Ensure you make their differences heard to give character to your playing. Prepare for this song with
Warm-up 7 on page 11.

Yankee Doodle

Traditional Anglo-American

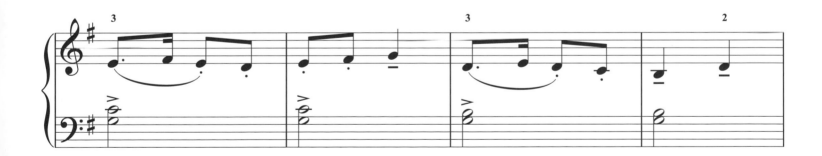

Watch out for the octave leaps in the left hand in measures 7 and 15, and the octaves played together in the second half of the piece. Practise these measures on their own to begin with.

Follow the dynamics carefully to enhance your performance.

Minuet in F

Leopold Mozart

Andantino grazioso

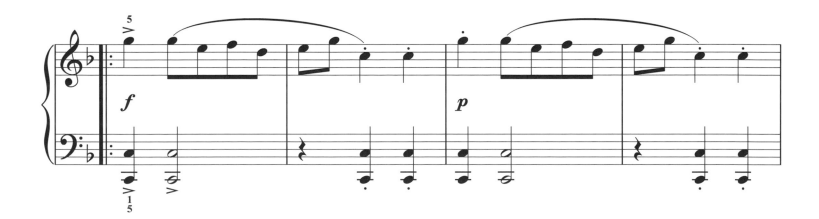

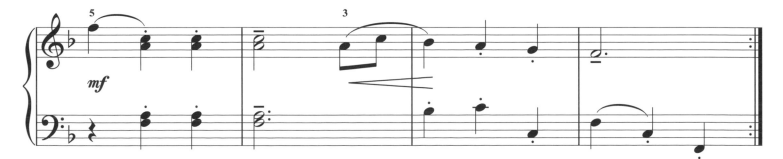

Practise the left-hand octave leaps in this warm-up before you play.

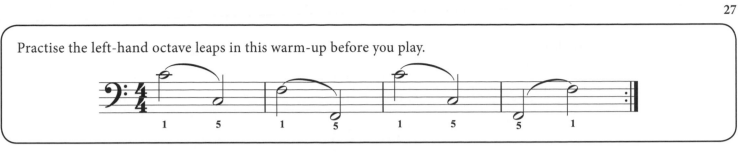

Melody

Daniel Gottlob Türk

At a walking pace

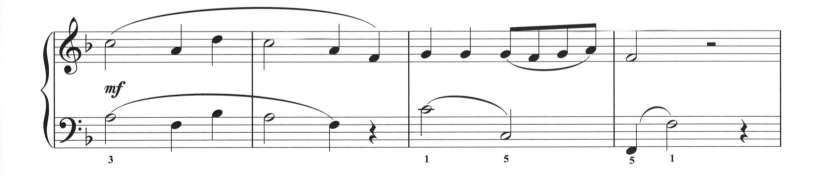

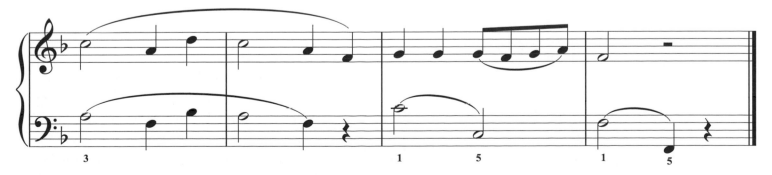

sf *sforzato* tells you to 'force' the sound, accenting them; **molto marcato** tells you to make the melody very accented; *sim.* **simile** tells you to continue playing in the same way — in this case, playing the left hand *staccato* throughout.

On page 29, there is a quarter-note rest above a bar line — take a pause here of a quarter-note's duration, before moving on to the next measure.

Country Dance
No.6 from FOR CHILDREN

Béla Bartók

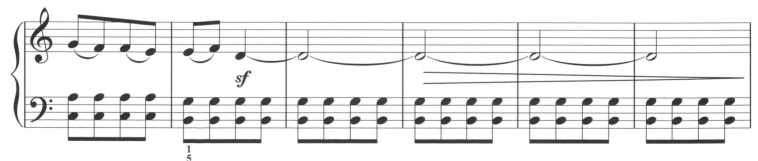

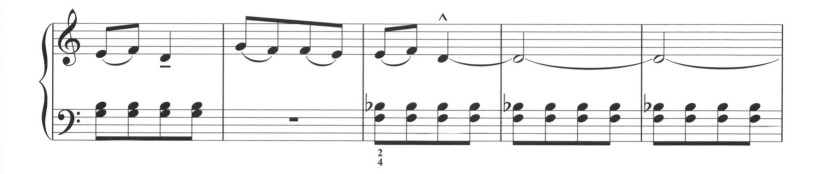

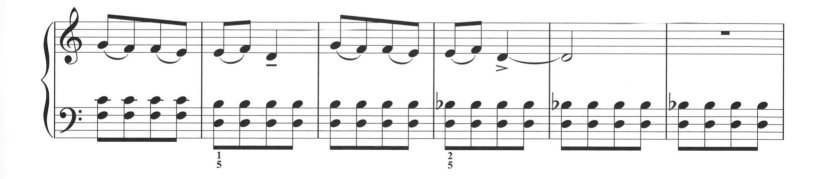

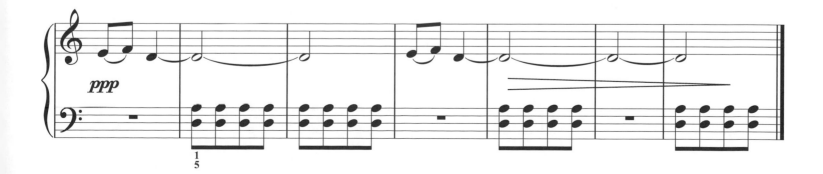

German Dance

Franz Joseph Haydn

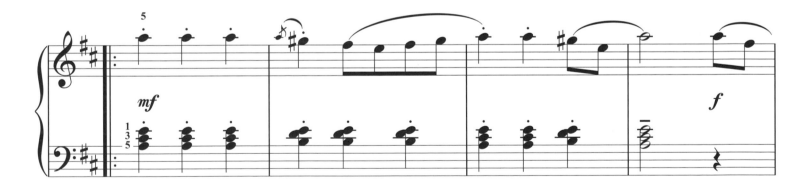

Watch out for the **accented staccato** notes—for example, in measure 6 (second system). These should be played as short, spiky notes with a heavy attack.

Also note the change of fingering on repeated notes of the same pitch, to help you with the quick succession.

The Song Of The Hussars

Louis Köhler

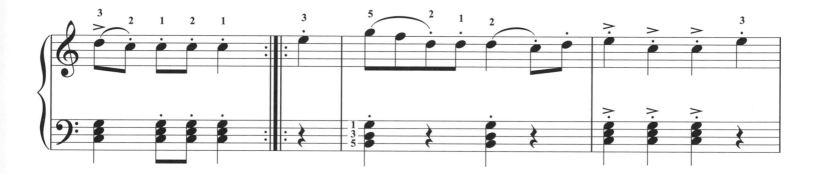

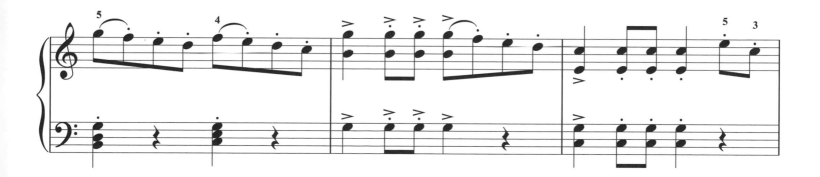

Watch out for the change of fingering on the repeated note D, to help you with the quick succession of notes.

William Tell Overture

Gioachino Rossini

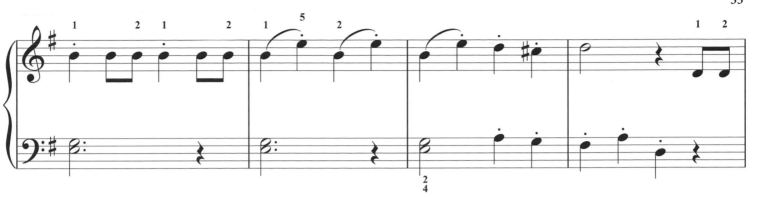

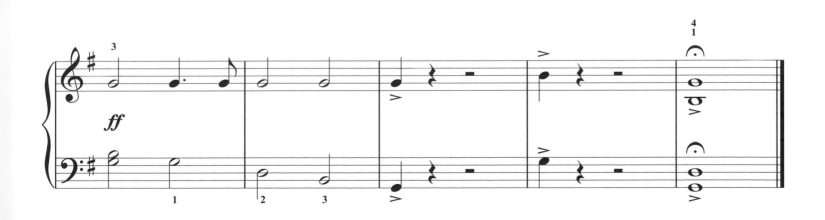

Your right hand moves around more here, so follow the fingering to help you change hand position.

The Can-Can
from ORPHEUS IN THE UNDERWORLD

Jacques Offenbach

Allegro

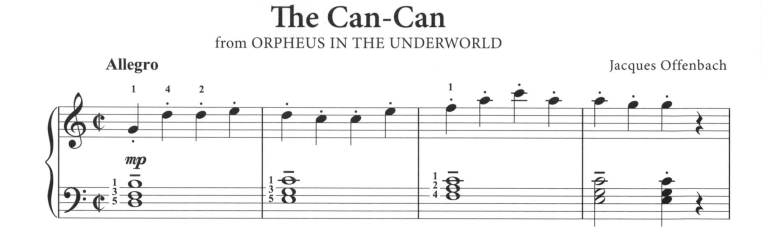

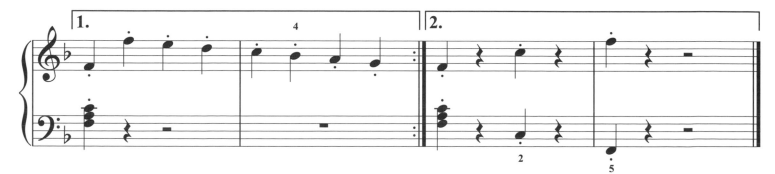

Little Suite

Daniel Gottlob Türk

Allegretto

Practise the sixteenth notes in the right hand to make sure you play them evenly at speed.

Where do you think the 'surprise' of its title is?

Surprise Symphony

(Symphony No. 94)

Franz Joseph Haydn

Andante

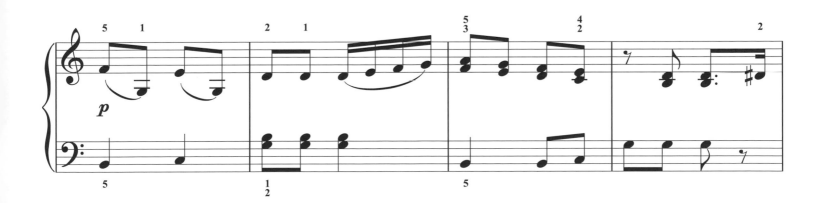

Play the left hand smoothly, contrasting it with the *staccato* in the right hand, which should be played crisply and lightly, with a bounce.

Raindrops

Jacob Schmitt

Allegretto

Watch out for the following rhythms: ♩. ♪ and *3* ♩♩♩, as well as some **syncopation**: ♪ ♩ ♪
Play the rhythms crisply and accurately.

Caro Nome
from RIGOLETTO

Giuseppe Verdi

Moderately

Look at the **time signature** at the start. It is known as **cut time** or **cut common time**—have a look at page 8 and 21 for a reminder.

The Caissons Go Rolling Home

E.L. Gruber

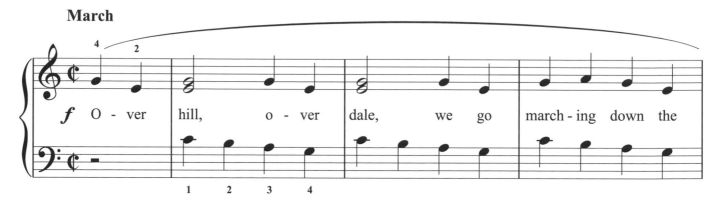

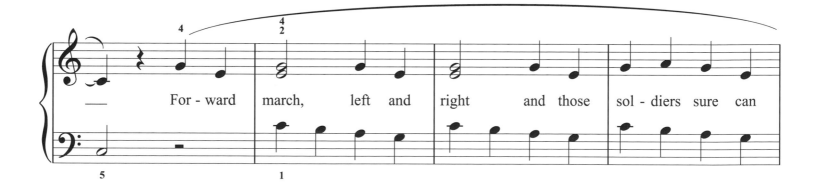

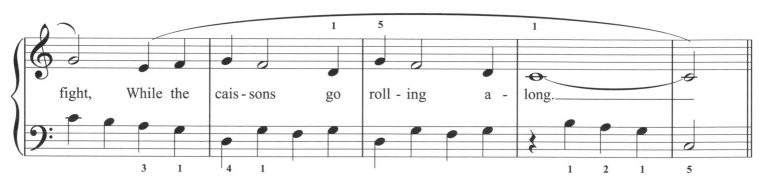

41

CHORUS

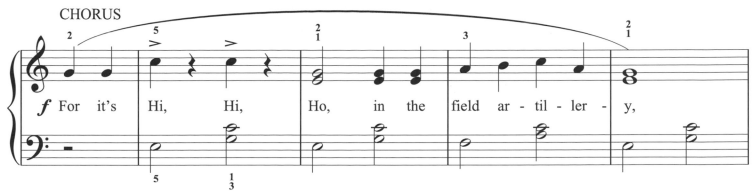

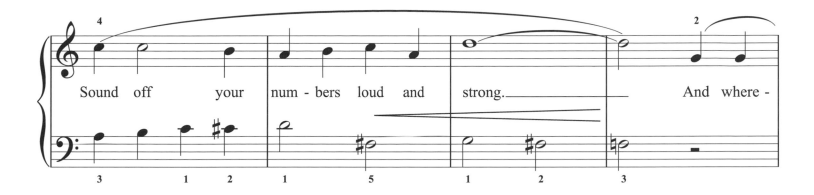

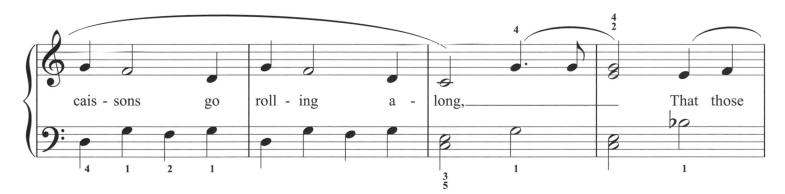

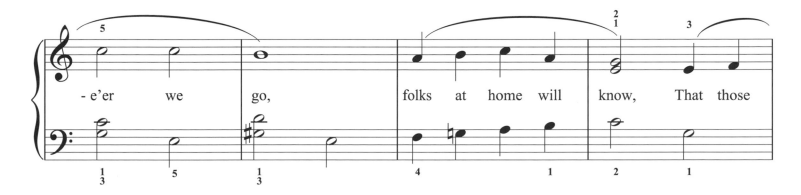

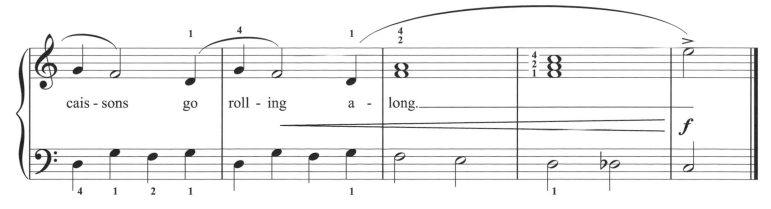

Sarabande in D minor

George Frideric Handel

Be prepared for the stretches in the right hand, each marked with an asterisk. Prepare using Warm-up 6 on page 10.

The Harmonious Blacksmith

George Frideric Handel

Gavotte

George Frideric Handel

Andante

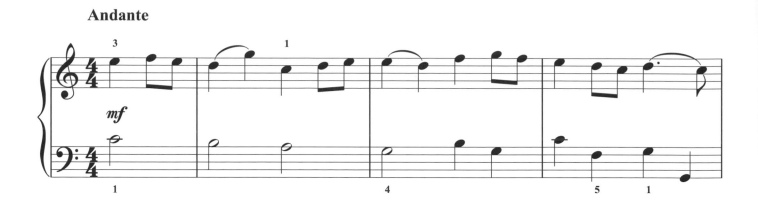

Russian Folk Dance

Ludwig van Beethoven

Vivace

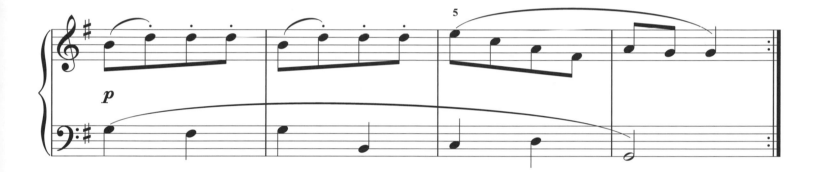

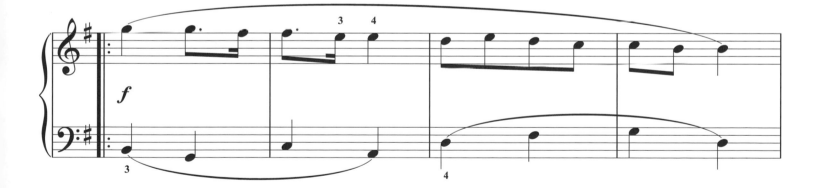

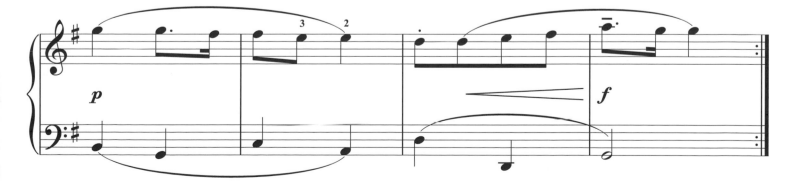

Minuet

Georg Philipp Telemann

Allegretto

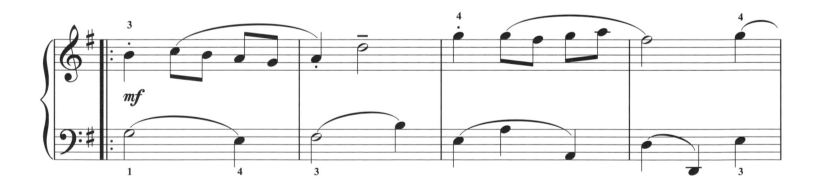

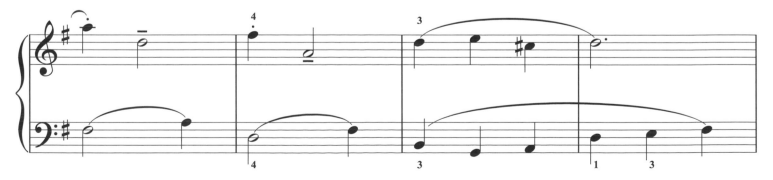

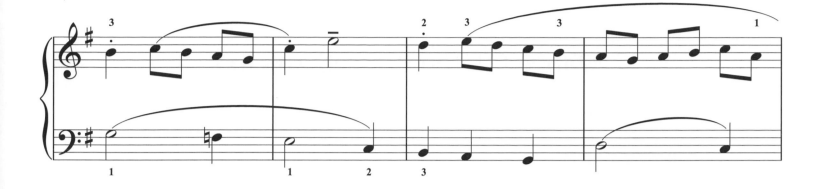

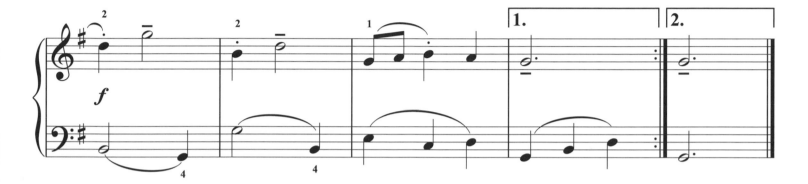

Gavotte

Georg Philipp Telemann

Moderately, with grace

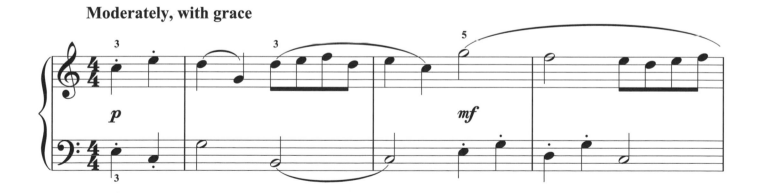

Watch out for the **accidentals** in this piece.

Dance Of The Blessed Spirits

Christoph Willibald Gluck

Lento

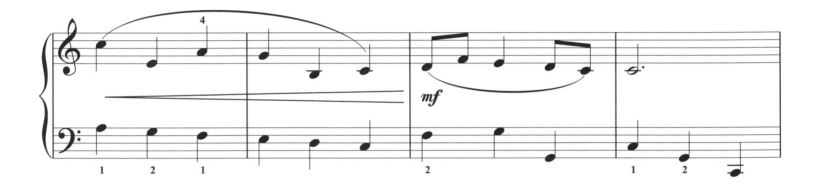

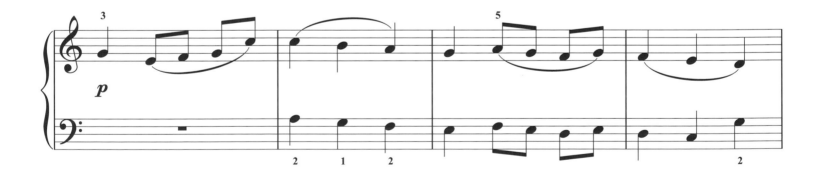

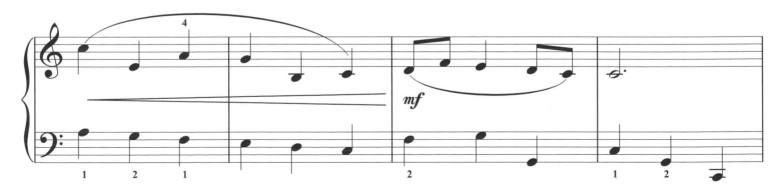

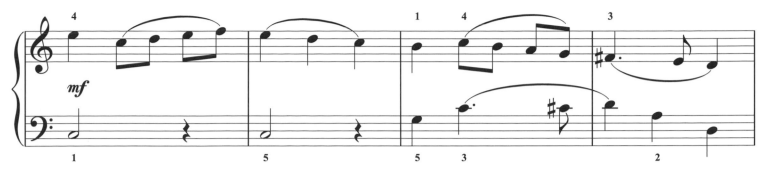

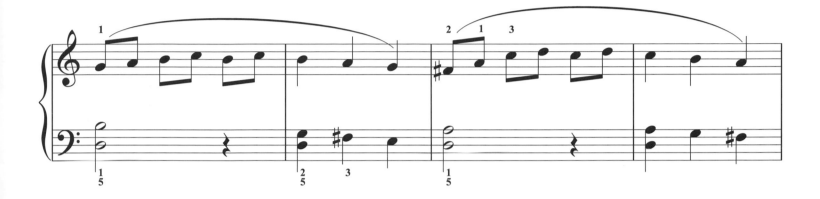

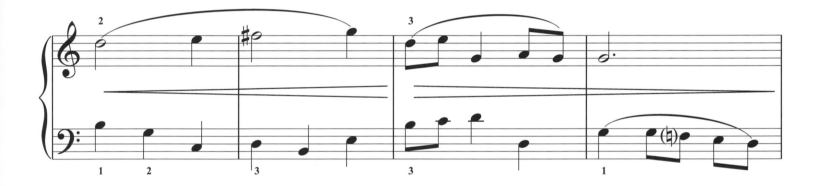

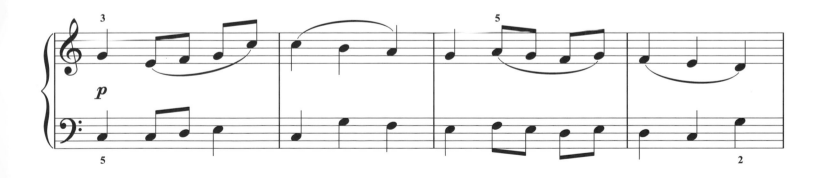

Make the ♩. ♪ rhythms nice and crisp. First practise hands together slowly before you build up to the **Allegro** tempo.

Autumn
from THE FOUR SEASONS (3rd movement)

Antonio Vivaldi

Frolic

Daniel Gottlob Türk

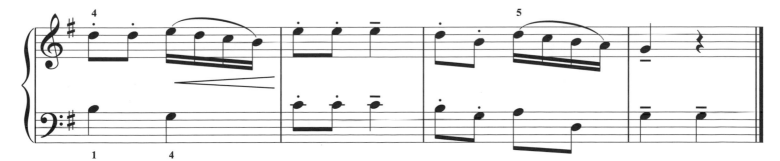

Watch out for the **tempo** changes and the **fermata** near the end.

Minuet in F, K. 2

Wolfgang Amadeus Mozart

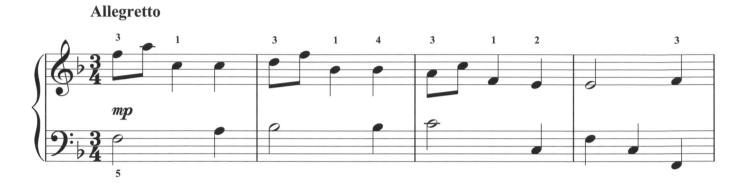

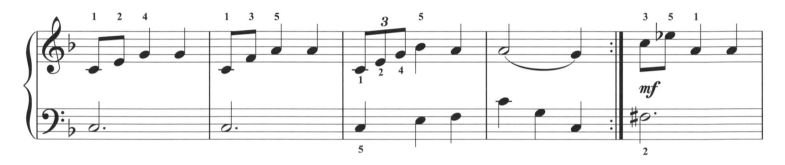

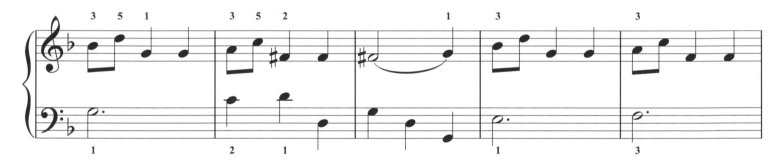

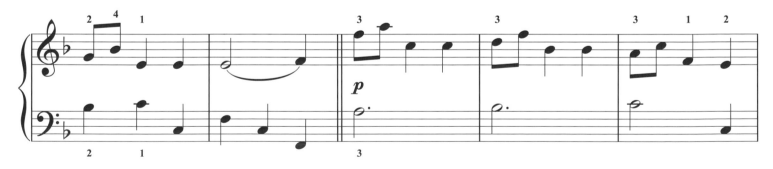

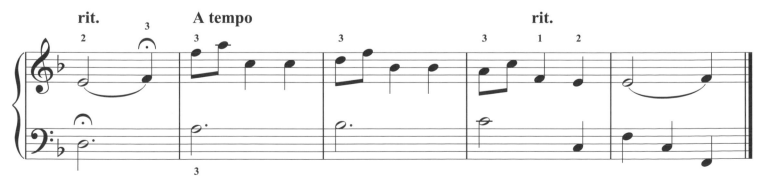

Look at the **key signature** — this is the key signature for B♭ major. Which notes should you play as flats?

Watch out for the **accidentals** — sometimes a natural sign is placed in front of a note to cancel the flat of the key signature.

Entr'acte from 'Rosamunde'

Franz Schubert

Andantino

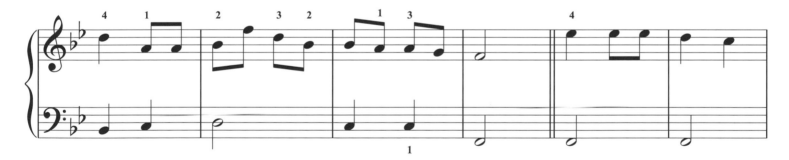

Minuet
from PARTITA No. 1

Johann Sebastian Bach

Moderato

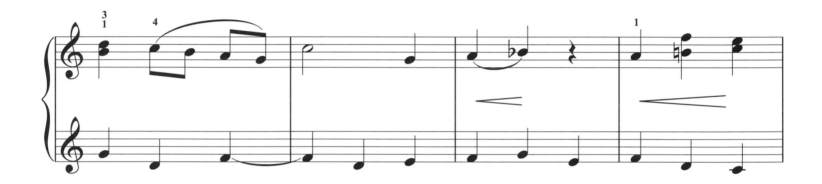

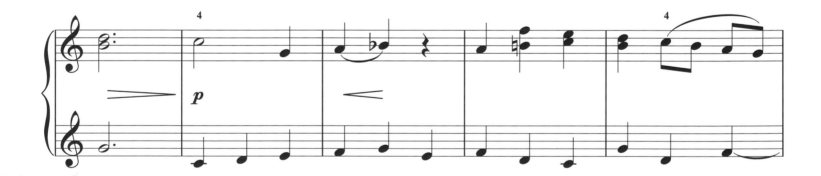

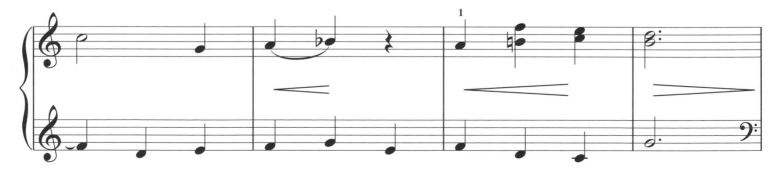

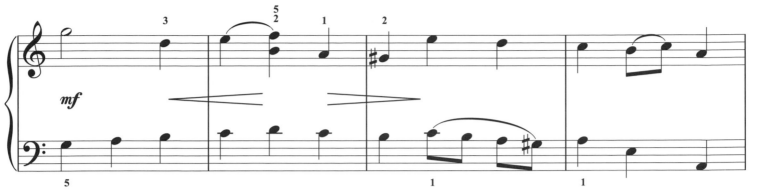

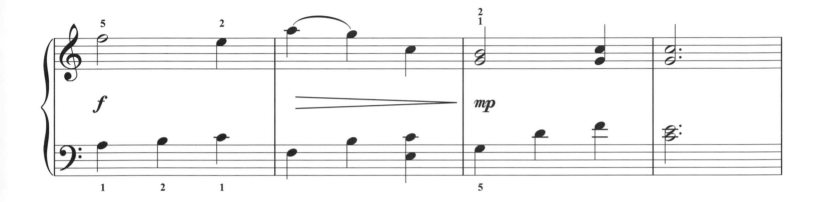

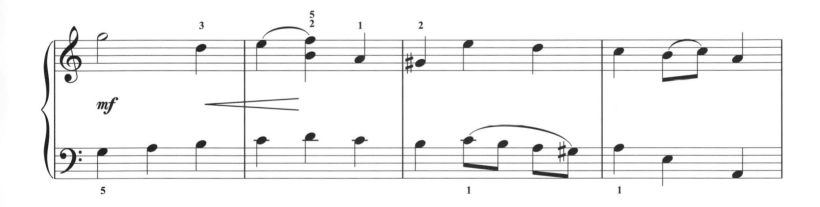

poco rit.

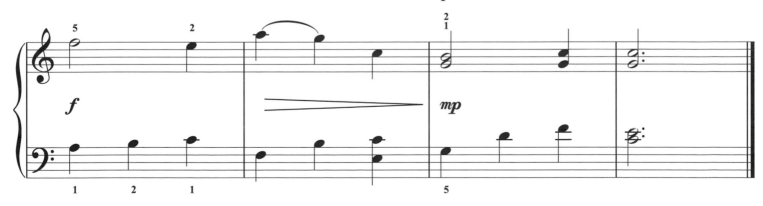

***tr* trill** — the brackets show that this is optional.

There are many different ways to execute trills, but this is one way you might interpret the one in this piece.

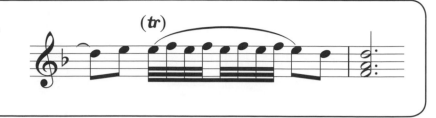

Largo

Arcangelo Corelli

Slowly and broadly

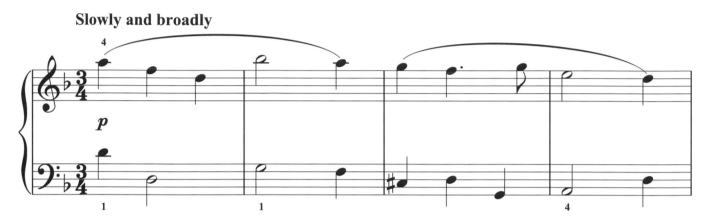

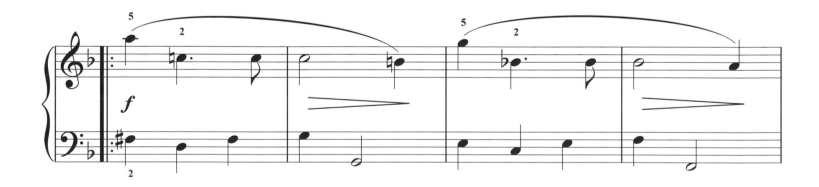

$\frac{6}{8}$ is a **compound meter** with two groups of three eighth notes in each measure.

Count "**1** **2**", or "**1** 2 3 **2** 2 3" in your head as you play.

Over The River And Through The Woods

Traditional American

There are two parts, or **voices**, in one hand at points in this piece. Use Warm-up 8 on page 11 to prepare.

Beautiful Heaven

Traditional Mexican

Moderately

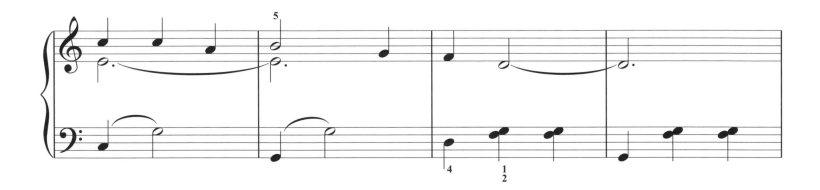

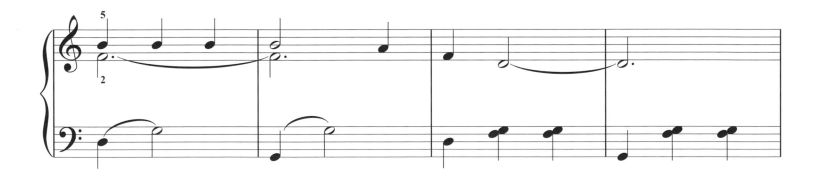

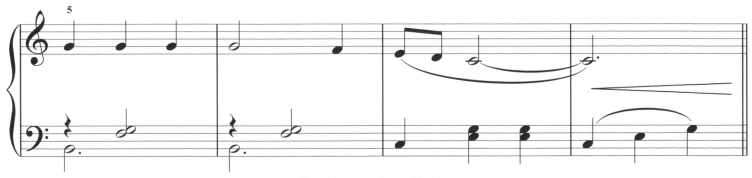

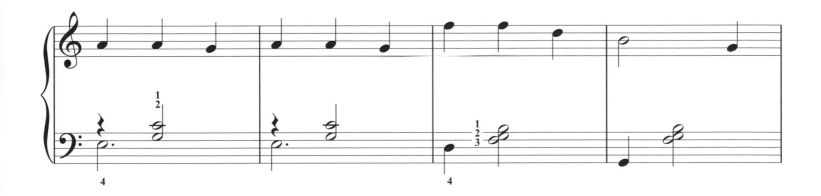

Red River Valley

Traditional American

Lively

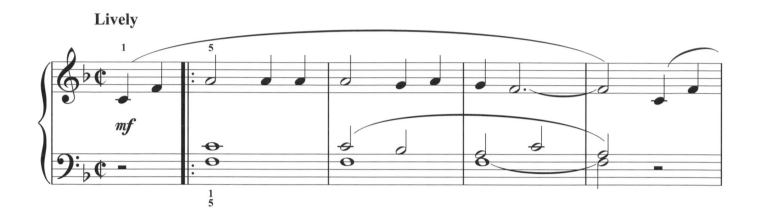

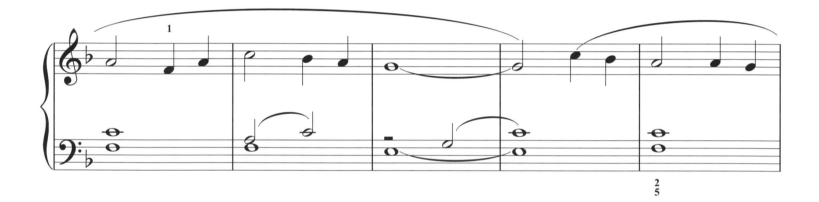

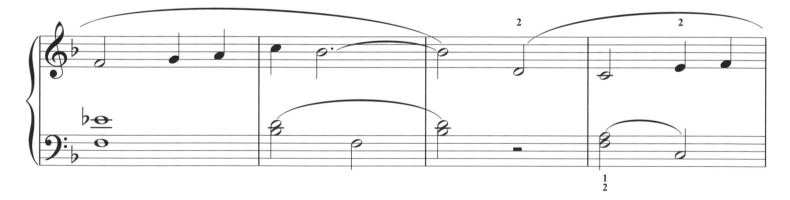

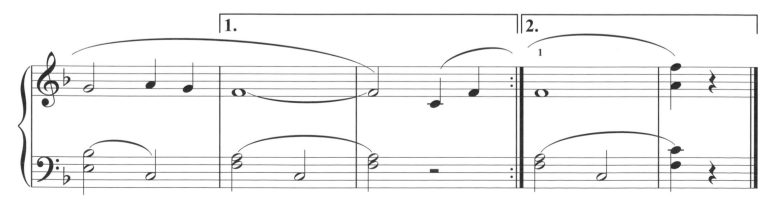

Sonata in A

(1st movement)

Wolfgang Amadeus Mozart

Andante grazioso

Watch out for the **accidentals** in this piece.

Für Elise

Ludwig van Beethoven

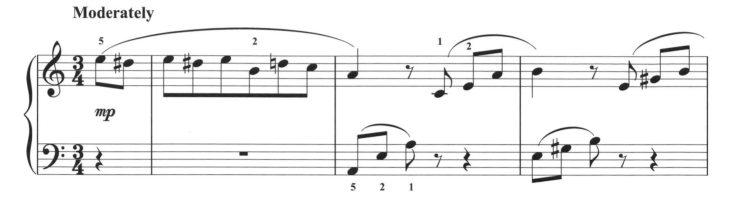

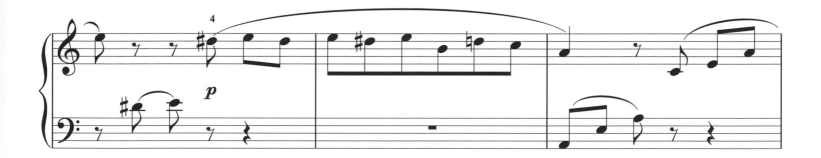

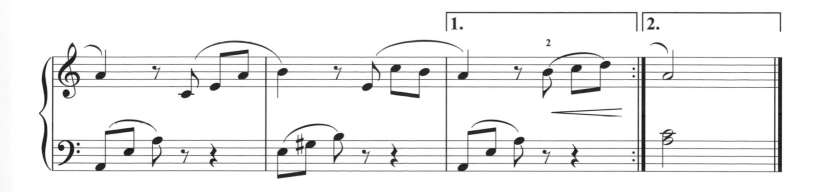

Watch out for the **caesura** // (also known as 'railroad tracks'). This indicates a break and short pause before playing on.

Hide And Seek

Robert Schumann

Allegro giocoso

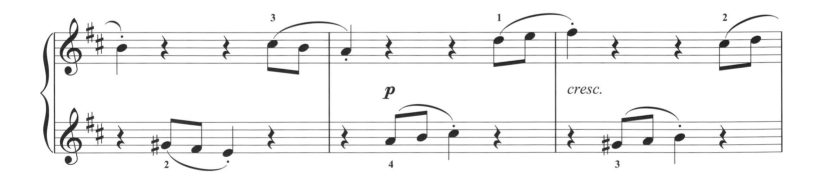

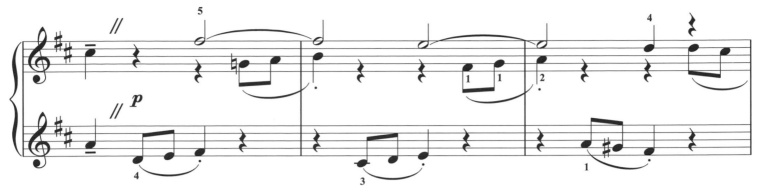

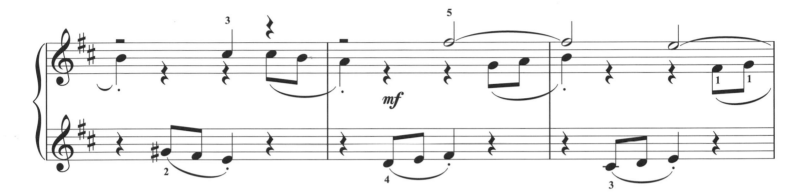

Playful Dialogue

Johann Nepomuk Hummel

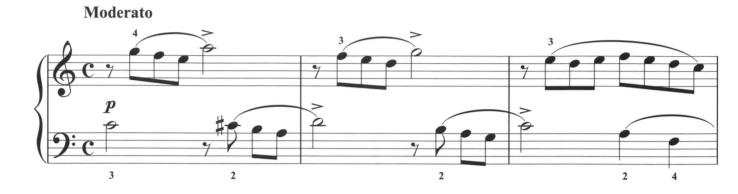

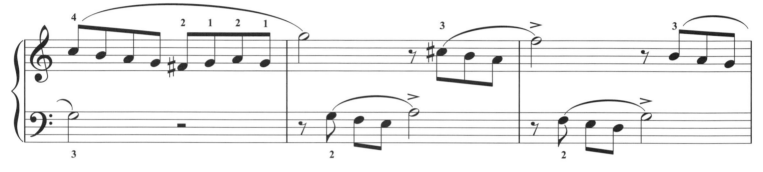

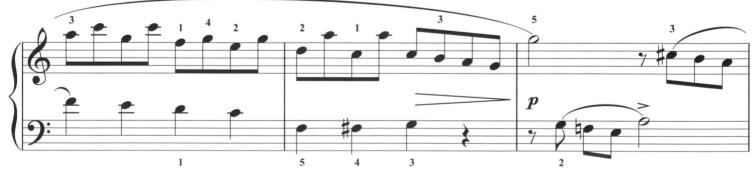

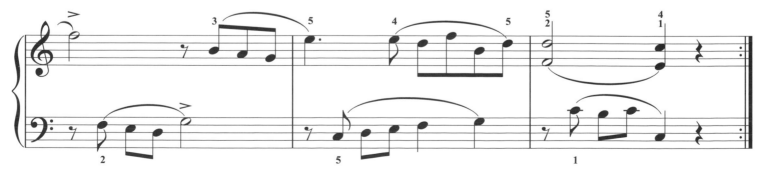

The Cuckoo

August Eberhard Müller

Allegretto

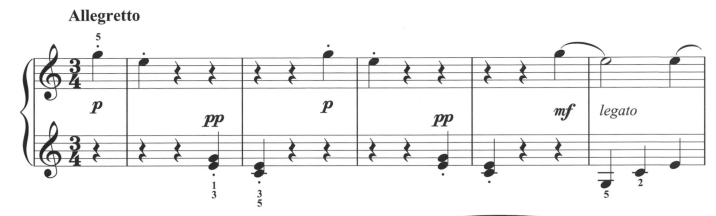

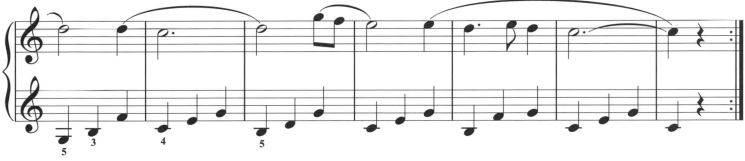

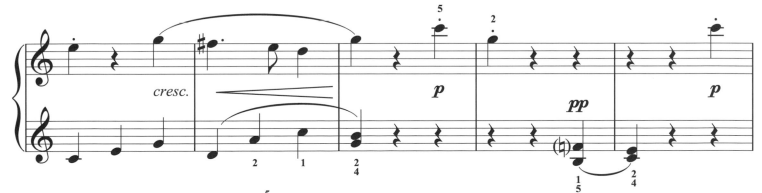

Bagatelle

Anton Diabelli

Allegretto

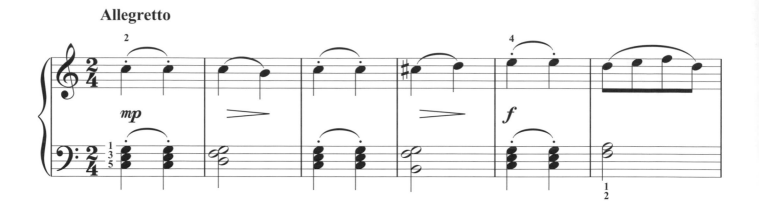

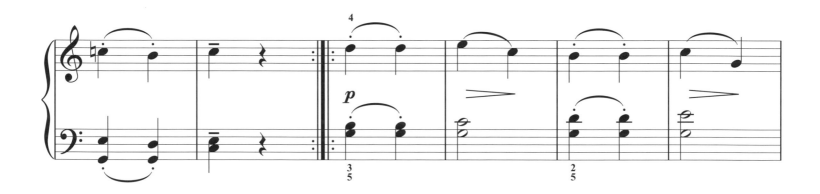

Little Song

Cornelius Gurlitt

Moderato

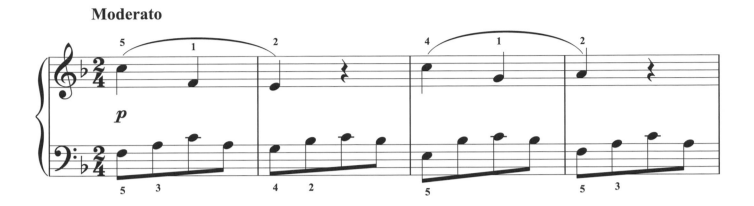

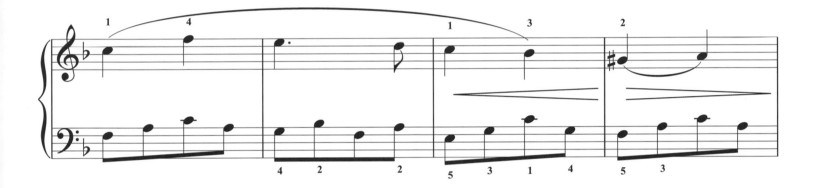

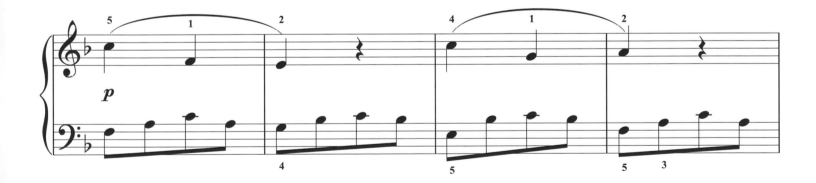

Your left-hand moves independantly to the right in this piece. Prepare for this by playing Warm-up 9 on page 11.

Little Piece

Robert Schumann

Moderato

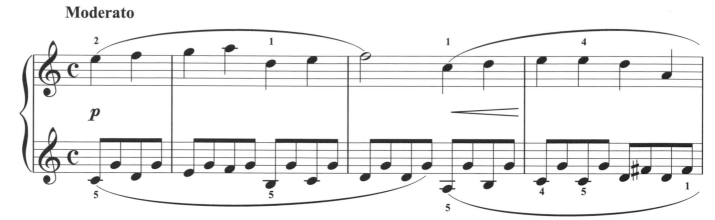

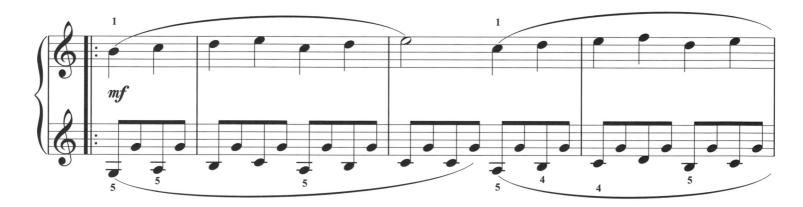

Look at the **key signature** — this is the key signature for D major. Which notes should you play as sharps?

Study in D

Carl Czerny

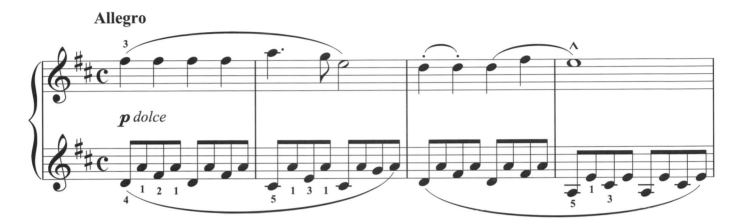

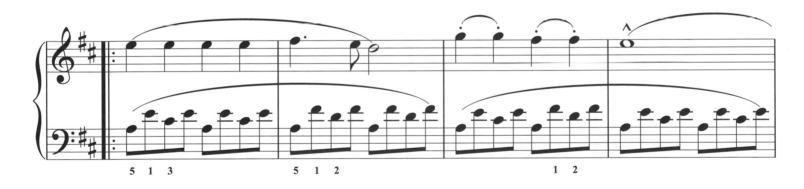

She'll Be Coming Round The Mountain

Traditional American

With a strong and steady beat

In A Little French Village

Pyotr Ilyich Tchaikovsky

With feeling

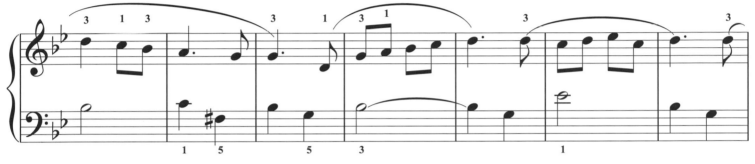

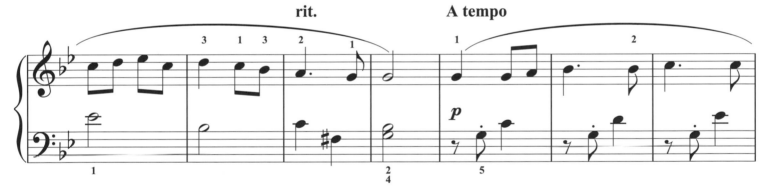

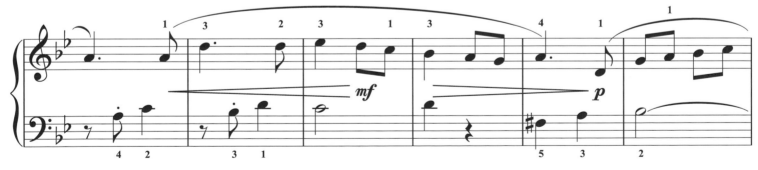

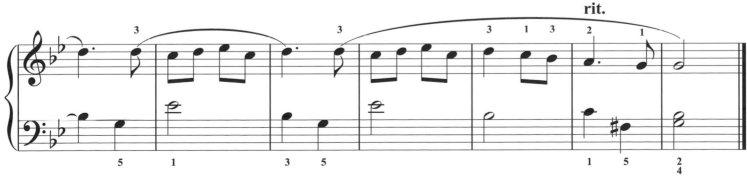

Arrival Of The Queen Of Sheba
from SOLOMON

George Frideric Handel

Allegro

Turkey In The Straw

Traditional American

Moderately fast

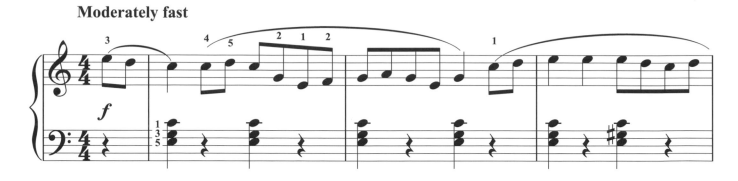

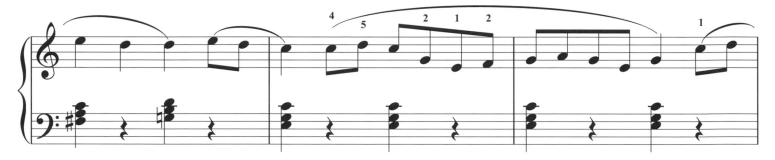

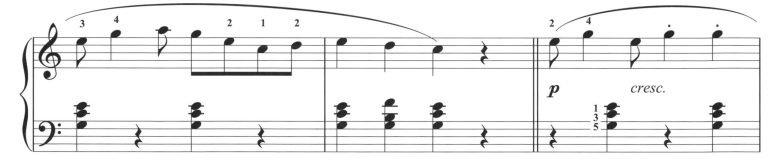

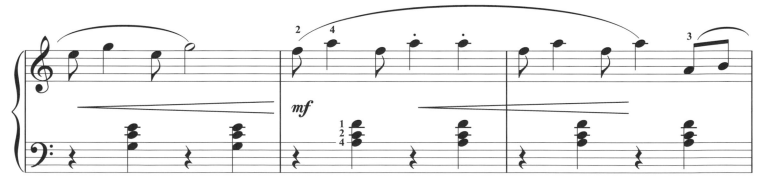

Country Minuet

Franz Joseph Haydn

Allegretto

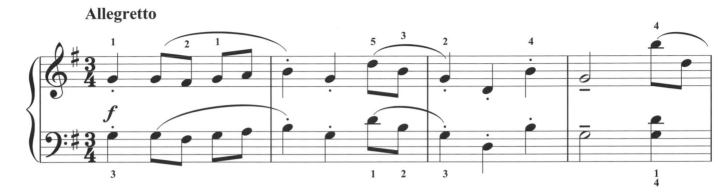

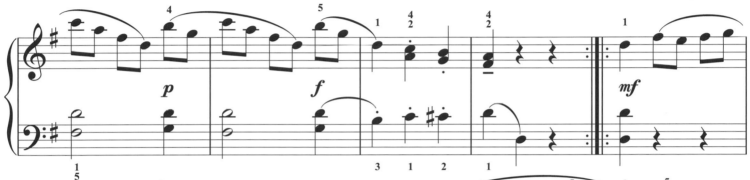

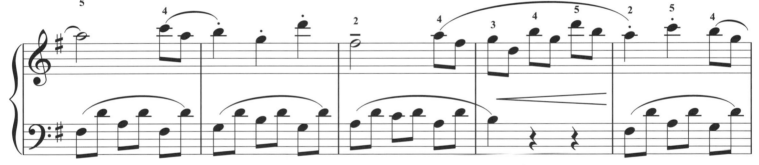

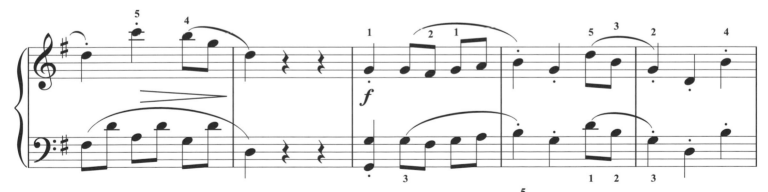

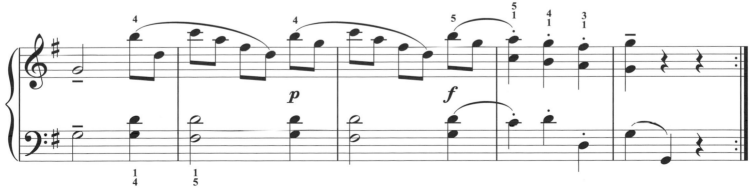

Prelude in A major

Frédéric Chopin

Andantino

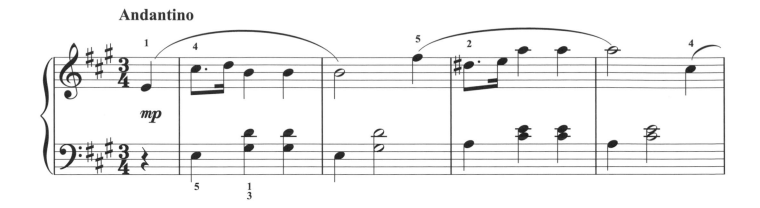

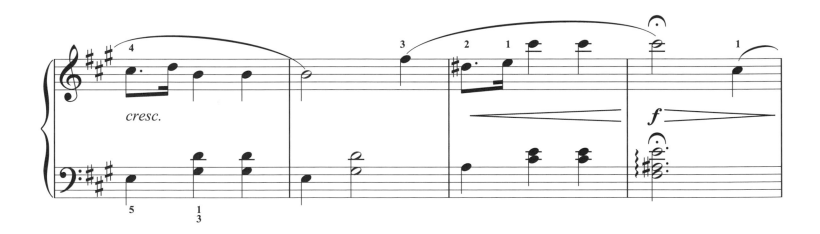

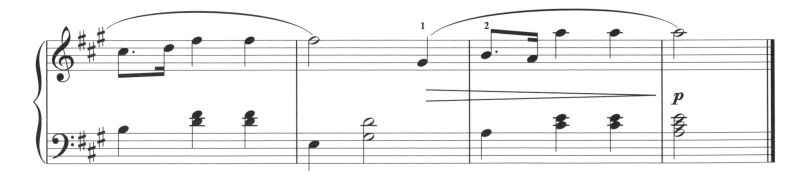

Bagatelle

Johann Nepomuk Hummel

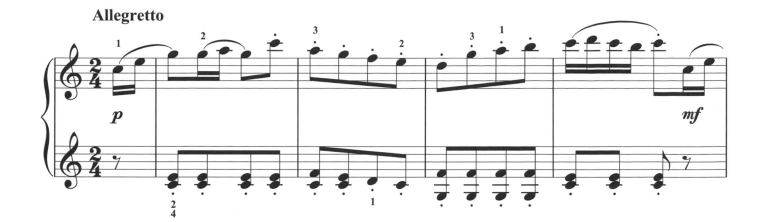

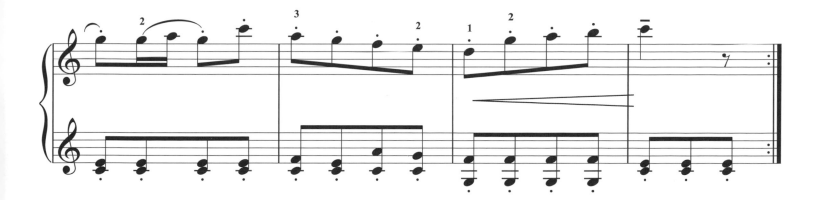

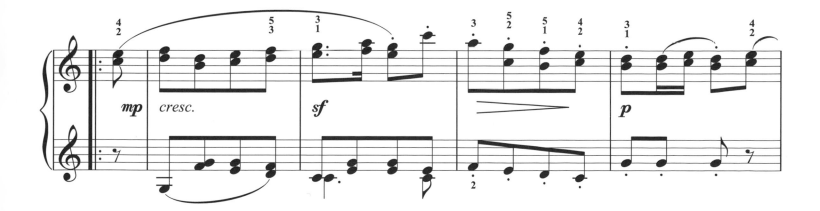

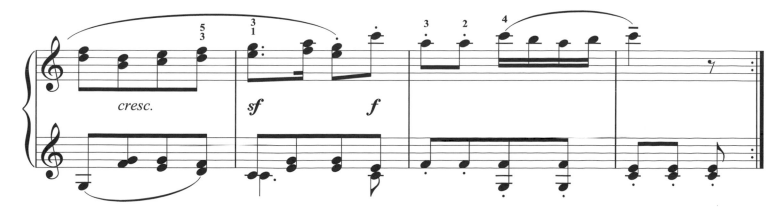

1 2 3 4 5 6 7 8 9

Published by
Yorktown Music Press/Music Sales Limited
14-15 Berners Street, London W1T 3LJ, UK.

Exclusive Distributors:

Music Sales Limited
Distribution Centre, Newmarket Road,
Bury St Edmunds, Suffolk IP33 3YB, UK.

Music Sales Corporation
180 Madison Avenue, 24th Floor,
New York NY 10016, USA.

Music Sales Pty Limited
4th floor, Lisgar House, 30-32 Carrington Street,
Sydney, NSW 2000, Australia.

Order No. YK22176
ISBN: 978-1-78558-242-4
This book © Copyright 2016 Yorktown Music Press,
a part of Music Sales Limited.

Compiled and edited by Lisa Cox, Sam Lung and Christopher Hussey.
Tutorial text by Christopher Hussey.
Music engraved and processed by Camden Music Services.
Printed in the EU.

Your Guarantee of Quality:

As publishers, we strive to produce every book
to the highest commercial standards.

This book has been carefully designed to minimise
awkward page turns and to make playing from it a real pleasure.

Particular care has been given to specifying acid-free, neutral-sized
paper made from pulps which have not been elemental chlorine bleached.
This pulp is from farmed sustainable forests and was produced
with special regard for the environment.

Throughout, the printing and binding have been planned to ensure
a sturdy, attractive publication which should give years of enjoyment.
If your copy fails to meet our high standards, please inform us
and we will gladly replace it.

www.musicsales.com